DARWIN'S THEORY OF EVOLUTION

The Origin of Species

Written by Romain Parmentier
Translated by Carly Probert

History

DARWIN'S THEORY OF EVOLUTION   1

Key information

POLITICAL, ECONOMIC AND SOCIAL CONTEXT   3

Britain all over the world
The century of science
Before Darwinism: Fixism vs. Transformism

BIOGRAPHIES   10

Charles Darwin
Alfred Russel Wallace

THE THEORY OF EVOLUTION   16

A voyage on board the *Beagle*
The time for questioning
The Galapagos Islands and their finches
Survival of the fittest
The Origin of Species by Means of Natural Selection

IMPACT   26

Religious and scientific opposition
Darwinism and Neo-Darwinism

SUMMARY   31

FIND OUT MORE   35

DARWIN'S THEORY OF EVOLUTION

KEY INFORMATION

- **When:** 24 November 1859
- **Where:** London
- **Context:** The scientific debate on the origin of species in the 19th century
- **Contributors:**
    - Charles Darwin, British naturalist (1809-1882)
    - Alfred Russel Wallace, British traveler and naturalist (1823-1913)
- **Impact:**
    - New conception of the origin of species in natural history
    - Creation of Darwinism

On 24 November 1859, the book entitled *On the Origin of Species by Means of Natural Selection, or the Preservation of Favoured Races in the Struggle for Life* first appeared. The book, which has been reprinted several times and translated into many languages, upset public opinion in the 19th century. Its author, Charles Darwin, asserted that all species that inhabit the Earth are the result of a slow evolution and that they continue to evolve in a desperate struggle for survival. But are these species not immutable beings, living in a bountiful nature according to the will of God? The gap between these two ideas is striking.

It took many years for Charles Darwin to transcribe his thoughts and his theory. Fascinated by the natural sciences, it was primarily his trip as a naturalist aboard the *Beagle* which laid the foundations for his revolutionary ideas. After departing in December 1831, the ship returned to England in October 1836. During these five years, the young scientist took the opportunity to collect and study a multitude of animal and plant species. He also underwent a series of experiences that changed his view of nature forever.

Upon his return, Charles Darwin collected his thoughts. In 1839, he came to the conclusion that the species undergo changes, allowing for an evolution by natural selection in the struggle for survival. Eaten away by anxiety at facing the consequences that such a scientific disruption could cause, Darwin took twenty years to complete his work, trying to provide answers for those who would contest it, and forever marked the history of the world.

POLITICAL, ECONOMIC AND SOCIAL CONTEXT

BRITAIN ALL OVER THE WORLD

The 19th century was undoubtedly the era of Britain. Indeed, the country that saw the birth of Charles Darwin was at its peak. Although its rise in power had been developing for many decades, it accelerated particularly in the late 18th and 19th centuries. Britain was the first to enter the industrial revolution of iron, coal and the steam engine, giving it the opportunity to get ahead of all other nations. Industry then considerably developed the British economy, and Britain exported more and more goods, to the point of becoming the world's largest economy.

Another factor that also marks the importance of 19th century Britain is the significance of its territories. At the end of the previous century, when the country lost its American colonies following the War of Independence (1775-1783), it nevertheless still possessed Canada and many territories in the Caribbean. Strengthening the power of its navy, Britain inexorably continued its territorial conquests. Many expeditions allowed it to take possession of Australia, New Zealand, and many islands in the Pacific. In addition, India, which had been so coveted by all the European countries, was gradually conquered by the British between 1757 and 1858, when the territory definitively passed under the authority of the Crown. Finally, Africa was the subject of a fierce struggle among the European powers in the second half of the 19th century. There, Britain carved a true empire for itself, with colonies extending from Cairo to Cape Town.

Britain's control of the seas also resulted from its victories over European rivals, starting with France. After the wars of the French Revolution and the Napoleonic Wars (1793-1815), the British finally took the French and Spanish competitors out of the race, turning the country into the first maritime power. The 1815 Treaty of Vienna also granted Britain a series of fortified bases, such as Gibraltar, Freetown (Sierra Leone), St. Helena, Cape Town, Mauritius, Ceylon and Malta, which henceforth served to ensure communication between the colonies and the metropolis.

THE CENTURY OF SCIENCE

Inherited from the Enlightenment, whose objective was to fight Obscurantism, the enthusiasm for scientific research continued and accelerated in a 19th century that was both romantic and positivist.

Based on the work of the father of modern chemistry, Lavoisier (1743-1794), to whom we owe the first isolation of chemical elements, his successors discovered almost all the elements in the 19th century. In 1869, Russian chemist Mendeleev (1834-1907) classified them according to their atomic weights in his famous periodic table.

The field of electricity even experienced its first success with the invention of the battery by Alessandro Volta (Italian physicist, 1745-1827) in 1800. Many other discoveries resulted from this invention, such as the principle of electrolysis revealed by Anthony Carlisle (British physiologist, 1768-1840) and electromagnetism discovered by André Marie Ampere (French physicist, 1775-1836) and Michael Faraday (British chemist and physicist, 1791-1867).

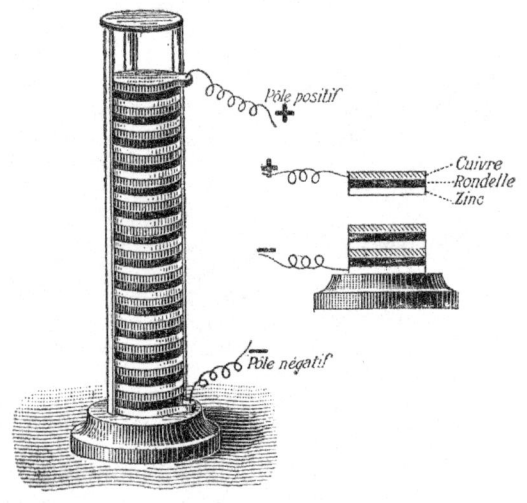

Voltaic pile, image from the book *Leçons de Physique de Louise* by Margat-L'Huillier. Paris: Vuibert et Nony, 1904.

In medicine, anesthesia began to be more widely used in 1844 thanks to ether. Progress also continued in the field of antibiotics and vaccines, particularly with the work of Louis Pasteur (French chemist and biologist, 1822-1895).

This thirst for knowledge also pushed European intellectuals to explore the different regions of the world in order to understand how it worked. These large scientific expeditions included cartographers, who were responsible for continually improving the maps of remote areas, astrologers who, through their observations, expanded the knowledge of the universe, but also many naturalists who collected and continually discovered animal and plant species. The primary objective was not so much the discovery of new territories anymore, but the deepening of the understanding of the world and everything in it.

BEFORE DARWINISM: FIXISM VS. TRANSFORMISM

Until the early 19th century, one idea dominated all: creationism. Following the biblical precepts of Genesis, all species were considered immutable, having emerged spontaneously and independently of each other according to the will of God. In addition, the geological time scale of the time was quite different from the one we know today. Indeed, it traced the creation of the Earth on Sunday 23 October 4004 B.C., which would not have allowed for the theory of evolution as we know it today as it was such a short time ago. This deeply religious trend was relayed in the scientific world by Fixism, which states that each species has crossed the ages without changing, or at least without undergoing any significant changes. Fixism gained importance in the 18th century with the work of Carl Linnaeus (Swedish naturalist and physician, 1707-1778), who designed a species classification system by assigning each individual a Latin name, a gender and a species. The system, which is still used today, was then considered to be fixed and immutable, reflecting the original division desired by the Creator.

Carl Linnaeus, engraving from the book *Famous Men of Science* by Sarah K. Bolton. New York: T. Y. Crowell & Co., 1889.

A TIMED CALCULATION

The date of the creation of the world (Sunday 23 October 4004 B.C.) was calculated in the 17th century by the Irish Archbishop James Ussher (1581-1656). He established its chronology based on the Bible, which tells the entire male line from Adam, the first man, to Solomon (King of Israel, 970-931 B.C.), considering the age mentioned of each descendant. He then made the connection with the chronology of the Kings of Israel, and with perfectly datable events occurring at that time in other civilizations, such as the Romans. It was this counting down that eventually led to the year of 4004 B.C. The month and year were then determined based on the beginning of the Jewish year, which was 23 October for that year. The day of Sunday was also chosen according to Jewish tradition. According to Genesis, God created the world in six days and rested on the seventh day, which for the Jews, corresponds to Saturday, Shabbat. The beginning of creation was therefore a Sunday, the first day of the Jewish week.

In the early 19th century, it was the French naturalist Georges Cuvier (1769-1832) who embodied the Fixist trend. Paradoxically, he was one of the scientific founders of the two disciples that underpinned the evolutionary theories a few decades later, namely paleontology (the study of living things from fossils) and comparative anatomy (kinship studies based on anatomy). However, despite the discovery of hundreds of fossils, Georges Cuvier positioned himself as a defender of Fixism, believing that the fossilized species had no connection with those of his time. He believed that some had disappeared and others had been created, completely independently. To support his hypothesis, he used a theory invoking great cataclysms, the latest of which was the flood overcome by Noah's ark.

Although Fixism dominated, another scientific trend dating back to the Antiquity became more and more significant at that time: transformism. Unlike Fixists, Transformists believed that species had changed over time in response to certain circumstances. Relayed by the great naturalists of the Enlightenment, such as Georges Louis Leclerc de Buffon (1707-1788), Transformism really saw its influence increase with Jean-Baptiste Lamarck (French naturalist, 1744-1829). For the latter, species undergo changes in a constant progression towards more complexity and advancement. He even made a law – which is now obsolete – concerning the inheritance of traits, stating that the transformation of an organ is passed down from generation to generation, changing species. The best-known example to support his claim was the giraffe, forced to feed on tree leaves, which gradually extended its neck. The transformation then became hereditary. Although genetics in the 20th century demonstrated that transformations and mutations of species are much more complex, Jean-Baptiste Lamarck nevertheless remains a precursor of the theory of evolution.

BIOGRAPHIES

CHARLES DARWIN

A naturalist and founder of the theory of evolution, Charles Darwin was born on 12 February 1809 in Shrewsbury (England) into a wealthy and educated family. Indeed, his grandfathers were physician, botanist, zoologist and poet Erasmus Darwin (1731-1802) and renowned potter Josiah Wedgwood (1730-1795), and his father, Robert Waring Darwin (1766-1848), was a doctor. Despite these excellent family careers, Charles Darwin had very little interest in school, which was reflected in his grades. However, he was passionate about nature and began to collect plants and insects from a young age.

Charles Darwin at age 7, by Ellen Sharples, 1816.

In 1825, when he was 16 years old, his father decided to send him to the University of Edinburgh to learn medicine. But these studies bored and even disgusted the young man, who left two years later. Nonetheless, it was there that he received his first lessons in Natural History, which confirmed his passions for botany and zoology. As the young Darwin seemed to be lacking a true calling, his father suggested that he become a pastor, but this position involved obtaining a diploma. Charles Darwin began three years of study at Cambridge, without much enthusiasm, but with the opportunity to take botany classes. He then befriended Professor John Henslow (British botanist and geologist, 1796-1861).

In 1831, he finally obtained his Bachelor of Arts degree and, on the advice of his professor, he took part in an expedition with Adam Sedgwick (1785-1873) to northern Wales shortly after. This experience perfected the naturalist training of Charles Darwin who, in addition to botany and zoology, was now familiar with geology.

On leaving university, he did not want to become a pastor. Instead, he dreamed of adventure and travel, like the great naturalists of his time. Again, John Henslow advised the young man and suggested he join the expedition of the HMS *Beagle* as a naturalist, going so far as to send letter of recommendation to the ship's captain, Robert FitzRoy (1805-1865). Charles Darwin was finally chosen and boarded the ship in December 1831, after managing to obtain the approval of his unwilling father. Although the trip was planned to last two years, five years were required for the

Beagle to fulfill its mission. This trip was decisive for Darwin who, through observing, collecting and analyzing all the species of plants, animals and minerals he found, began to formulate the theory which would later make him famous.

Back in England, he realized that he had become known within scientific circles. John Henslow had indeed taken care to publish the travel correspondence of the young naturalist. With this support, Charles Darwin saw the possibility to earn a living from his scientific research and definitively abandoned his career as a clergyman. In 1839, he married, entered the Royal Society and published his travelogue from the *Beagle*, which included a theory on the formations of atolls.

In 1858, another naturalist named Alfred Russel Wallace sent him his work on a theory of evolution that was similar to his own. Under pressure from his friends, Darwin finally decided to publish his work so as to get ahead of Wallace. On 24 November 1859, the book *On the Origin of Species by Means of Natural Selection, or the Preservation of Favoured Races in the Struggle for Life* was released in bookstores. Success was immediate.

Following this publication, the entire field of biology was turned upside down and intense debates took place within the scientific community. However, Charles Darwin, staying away from the controversy, continued to devote himself to his research, publishing numerous other writings and refining his theory. He died on 19 April 1882, in Down, Kent.

ALFRED RUSSEL WALLACE

Alfred Russel Wallace, 1908.

Alfred Russel Wallace was a naturalist born on 8 January in Usk (Wales). Fascinated by the natural sciences, from 1848 to 1852 he undertook travels to South America where, like other naturalists, he collected, observed and explored all kinds of species. He then set out again in 1854 to the Malay Archipelago and was based mainly in Borneo.

Following his observations, like Charles Darwin he soon came to the conclusion that animal and plant species are the result of a long evolution, of which natural selection is the driving force. Wishing to confront his ideas, he sent his work *On the Tendency of Varieties to Depart Indefinitely from Original Type* to Darwin in 1858. Seeing how advanced the work of Alfred Wallace was, Darwin, pushed by his friends, decided to publish his own theory as soon as possible. While recognizing the precedence of the work of Charles Darwin, Alfred Wallace continued to serve the theory of evolution throughout his life.

He died on 7 November 1913 in Broadstone (England).

THE THEORY OF EVOLUTION

A VOYAGE ON BOARD THE *BEAGLE*

Charles Darwin had barely finished his studies when he was offered the opportunity to participate in a scientific expedition of the British Admiralty on the *Beagle*. Commanded by Captain Robert FitzRoy, the mission aimed to continue the mapping of Patagonia and Tierra del Fuego, which had begun in 1826, and then conduct surveys on the coasts of Chile, Peru and some Pacific islands.

He boarded the *Beagle* and set off on Wednesday 27 December 1831, for a period of five years. Aged 22 at the time of departure, the naturalist later claimed that "the voyage of the Beagle [was] by far the most important event in [his] life and...determined [his] whole career" (Darwin, 2002).

Despite suffering from seasickness, the young naturalist enjoyed his mission on the *Beagle*. The commander allowed him to carry out long excursions to the shore so that he could explore, collect, study and naturalize all the species that were available to him. After several stops and a long Atlantic crossing, the ship arrived in the Bay of Rio on 4 April 1832. There, a stop of two months was planned, which gave Darwin the complete freedom to venture into the rainforest.

Fascinated by the incredible diversity at work in nature, the young man was also taken in by the chaos of the forest, where life stood side by side with death and decay, as well as by the fierce struggle between the species to try to survive. This sight was new for him. Until then, everyone considered the rainforest to be a magnificent Garden of Eden, where nature was good, according to divine will. But there, the naturalist discovered the opposite. Survival governed the behavior of individuals in this hostile environment. Darwin tirelessly began a general survey of living conditions of species and the connections between them.

THE TIME FOR QUESTIONING

The *Beagle* resumed its voyage on 5 July and arrived in Bahia Blanca (south of Buenos Aires) on 7 September. During a field trip, Charles Darwin discovered fossilized bones. Although he had already seen some, this was the first opportunity he had to examine them in their natural resting place. He then noticed that the bones were positioned in different geological layers, demonstrating a soil heave. However, his attention remained focused on the remains of the giant mammal, which surprisingly had similarities to other species that were still alive, while the precepts of Georges Cuvier stated otherwise. This mammal, which was given the name of Megatherium, was actually a giant sloth that had been extinct for 11 000 years.

This discovery fascinated Charles Darwin and fueled his thoughts. Was there a link between the extinct and living species? Are the species of today the outcome of a transformation of the older species? For the naturalist, it was too early to answer such questions. Nevertheless, his ever-growing discoveries and collections, which he shipped to England as soon as the opportunity arose, changed all his previous conceptions of the world and of nature.

In December 1832, a new experience came to upset naturalistic ideas even more. The *Beagle* reached Tierra del Fuego and was about to debark a missionary and three Fuegians (inhabitants of Tierra del Fuego). They had been brought to England to be educated three years before. The aim of the experiment was to bring them back to their original tribe to civilize the rest of the population. Although this part of the mission ended in total failure, it greatly served the reflections of the naturalist. Charles Darwin, who met "primitive" men for the first time, was appalled. He noted their basic way of life, their behavior which bordered on savagery and their struggle to survive in a precarious environment. However, three of them had been educated, which proved that there was no intellectual superiority, as many thought at the time, between "races" of men. Therefore, it was the environment that influenced the human condition. Faced with the spectacle of wild populations around the world, Charles Darwin observed that the boundary between man and animal was thinner than theologians wanted to believe. On the contrary, Darwin did not see man as a divine creation placed above everything, but a mammal among many others.

The HMS Beagle in Tierra del Fuego by Conrad Martens.
This painting was produced during the *Beagle*'s journey
(1831-1836).

After several trips and stops in Patagonia, the *Beagle* passed
the Strait of Magellan in June 1834. On 23 July, it reached
Valparaiso, Chile. Charles Darwin embarked on an initial
excursion to the Andes and, much to his astonishment,
discovered fossilized shells at 4 000 meters altitude. This
troubling experience made him realize that the soil had
been strongly raised by unknown forces. Moreover, such an
event must have occurred over a long period of time, which
called into question his ideas of geological time from the
Bible. The *Beagle* then went back down the coast to Valdivia
(port of Chile), reaching it in February 1835, before returning
to Valparaiso in March, where the naturalist explored the
Andes for a second time. In Valdivia, Charles Darwin faced
a violent earthquake, which made him realize the incredible

power of nature and, in particular, the instability of a constantly changing world.

THE GALAPAGOS ISLANDS AND THEIR FINCHES

After reaching Lima (Peru), the expedition headed to the Galapagos Islands, of which Charles Darwin was glad. This stage of the journey was indeed crucial for the naturalist in the development of his theory. The *Beagle* arrived on Chatham Island on 17 September 1835, and Darwin immediately began his exploration. Moving from island to island, he noticed that there were species in this archipelago that could not be found anywhere else. Among the most famous are the giant tortoises, of which he had the opportunity to taste the meat, and the iguanas, which he threw into the water several times to test their water resistance. Charles Darwin was also interested in the birds of the islands, namely the finches which, many years later, would become truly famous thanks to him.

Among the 26 species of land birds collected, the finches seemed quite ordinary at first glance. However, after observing them, Darwin distinguished no less than thirteen kinds of these small birds that were differentiated by the size of their beaks. They were sometimes very developed like a grosbeak, sometimes much thinner like a warbler, and between the two extremes was a multitude of sizes. Charles Darwin only realized the importance of the example of the finches much later, while he was developing his theory. They are indeed tangible evidence of the variations of species.

1. Geospiza magnirostris.
2. Geospiza fortis.
3. Geospiza parvula.
4. Certhidea olivacea.

Darwin's finches, 1845.

Likely to have descended from a common ancestor on the American continent, these birds have changed over time to suit the harshness of the environment of the Galapagos Islands. With food being limited, the species have evolved to include specific traits based on the food available on each island. Some have become seed-eaters, while others are insectivores. But even within the first category, individualities exist: indeed, some feed on harder, larger seeds, which only a stronger beak could split, while others feed on smaller seeds that are easier to eat, providing the necessary explanations as to the many types of beak that can be found on this bird.

Even today, "Darwin's finches" are studied to observe the

evolution of the species. Thus, during periods of drought, when food is less abundant, biologists are seeing a decline in the population of small-beaked finches, as they are not able to crack the larger seeds like the large-beaked finches, which can feed on everything. This discovery thus shows that the most adapted species will survive over the less adapted. Although Darwin did not speak of natural selection when he discovered the finches, he was nevertheless convinced of the variation of the species and speciation (formulation of new species).

With the *Beagle*'s mission coming to an end, the return to Britain could finally begin. On 20 October 1835, the vessel left the Galapagos and successively reached Tahiti, New Zealand and Australia. In April, it reached the Cocos Islands (Indian Ocean islands), where Darwin developed his theory on the formation of atolls. He was also fascinated by coral, whose various branches inspired his evolutionary trees (where the species go in multiple directions). Finally, after traveling through Mauritius, Cape Town, and the island of St. Helena, the ship arrived in Britain on 2 October 1836. During the trip, Charles Darwin had written 770 pages of notes and collected 1 529 species preserved in alcohol and 3 907 "dry" species. With such a vast basis of materials, the naturalist's reflection on his findings could continue for years.

SURVIVAL OF THE FITTEST

Upon his return, Charles Darwin noticed that he had become famous. His letters to John Henslow had indeed been read in scientific circles, therefore making him a known man of science. He immediately began cataloging his collections and even entrusted them to many experts, so as to get as much information as possible. In February 1837, the first results fell through, particularly on the Galapagos finches: there were 13 different types of finches, but they were all very close to one another. Meanwhile, Charles Darwin worked on his notes, which he eventually published in 1839. Finally, from July 1837 to July 1839, he wrote his first books on his theory of the origin of species.

However, Darwin remained cautious, aware that his ideas were dangerous for the time. Therefore, while remaining discreet, he surrounded himself with scientists, as well as stockbreeders, gardeners and nurserymen to collect new evidence. His theory now clearly differed from creationism, but also from the transformism of Lamarck. Thus, he hypothesized that the transformation of the species is not controlled the result of an animal's wish to improve, but rather an adaptation to its environment. Therefore, it was not the giraffes who stretched their own necks from eating leaves located in the trees, it was the giraffes with the longer necks that were able to have more food and thus survived. Through observation and reflection, Charles Darwin understood that this selection was the cornerstone of the transformation of species.

He thus noted that breeders of pets could identify minimal differences between certain animals and artificially select the most appropriate or the strongest to reproduce, thus gradually altering the species. In nature, this selection also occurs, but this is natural selection. However, Darwin did not yet understand how this selection took place naturally. What was the cause? Continuing his analysis, and especially his reading, he finally found the answer in *An Essay on the Principle of Population* by Thomas Malthus (British economist, 1766-1834), in which the human struggle for survival is presented. Remembering the fierce battle being fought by species in the rainforest, Charles Darwin realized the he had found the reason for natural selection: the struggle for survival. In a hostile environment, when living conditions of the environment are changing, only the most adapted will survive and reproduce, gradually transforming the species. The naturalist now had the basis of his theory, but his worry over the revolution that he would provoke constantly prevented the writing and publication of his book.

THE ORIGIN OF SPECIES BY MEANS OF NATURAL SELECTION

Charles Darwin wrote constantly over the next twenty years (1839-1859). He wrote works on atolls, volcanic islands and zoology from his voyage on the *Beagle*. In 1842 and 1844, he also wrote two drafts of his theory of evolution, but continued to tirelessly collect evidence before thinking about publishing it. Meanwhile, from 1846 to 1852, Darwin was devoted to studying barnacles (crustaceans) in order to further build his reputation, while continuing with his main work.

From 1856, Darwin began writing his book and in March 1858, ten chapters were completed, including the one dedicated to natural selection. Its actual publication was nevertheless hurried by an external element. Another naturalist, Alfred Wallace sent Darwin his own works, which proved highly similar to his own. Encouraged by his friends, Darwin presented a sample of his work on 1 July 1858 along with the essay of Alfred Wallace, but stated that he had been working on the theory since 1839. Although the essay was received with the greatest indifference, the naturalist continued writing his book. Finally, on 24 November 1859, he published his life's work: *On the Origin of Species by Means of Natural Selection, or the Preservation of Favoured Races in the Struggle for Life.*

An entirely new theory of evolution came to light. According to Charles Darwin, the species were not immutable as implied by creationism, but were the outcome of a slow process of evolution from a common ancestor. He stated that this change was governed by natural selection. For each species, changes may occur by chance. These can be positive of negative, depending on the circumstances (environment, climate, food, camouflage, etc.). Natural selection can then operate. If evolution is more suited to current circumstances, these individuals will then be more likely to survive and reproduce, thus passing on their specific traits to their offspring. The less suited are doomed to disappear. This change is therefore constant. It has neither direction, aim nor a specific purpose that would tend towards more progress, but is simply the result of better adaptation.

IMPACT

RELIGIOUS AND SCIENTIFIC OPPOSITION

The publication of *The Origin of Species* enjoyed immediate success, to the point where the first print run of 1250 copies was soon exhausted. There were six editions of the book by 1872, with extra information of revisions. Despite this success, the work raised many controversies. Made public by the newspaper, a real public debate began in Britain on the naturalist book between evolutionists and the Anglican Church, the latter being supported in the scientific world by the Fixists.

The work of Charles Darwin indeed aroused the wrath of the Church because it omitted or completely denied the existence of God. According to the conceptions of the time, all creation was the act of divine will, as taught in the Bible. Similarly, the image of a bountiful nature was completely undermined by Charles Darwin. Instead, he presented it as fierce, as it is the place where natural selection ruthlessly favors the fittest. Scientifically proving that no divine intervention was at the heart of the origin of species and their evolution, Charles Darwin invalidated the notion of God, and thus faith itself. Yet at the time, the Church saw itself as the guarantor of social order. The principle of evolution was even hostile to Fixists who had just completed the immutable classification of species according to the Linnaean system.

Finally, the work of Charles Darwin deliberately evaded

the question of man and his origins. The author hoped to avoid trouble, but his silence was quickly interpreted, and probably rightly so, as a wish to make no distinction between man and other species. Man is not above the fray, but is instead subject, like the other species, to the laws of evolution. This view was soon reduced to the idea that man evolved from apes – which Charles Darwin never claimed in his book.

The attacks from each side eventually led to a large debate that was held in Oxford on 30 June 1860. Darwin, then suffering, did not participate, but was represented by his friend, Thomas Huxley (British physiologist, 1825-1895), while the Bishop of Oxford, Samuel Wilberforce (1805-1873) spoke on behalf of the religious side. The debate between the two men was brutal. The bishop did not hesitate to ask his opponent if he had descended from apes through his grandfather. Thomas Huxley replied: "If then, said I, the question is put to me would I rather have a miserable ape for a grandfather or a man highly endowed by nature and possessed of great means of influence and yet who employs these faculties and that influence for the mere purpose of introducing ridicule into a grave scientific discussion, I unhesitatingly affirm my preference for the ape" (Continenza, 2004: 136). At the end of the debate, each side believed that he had gained the upper hand and so the controversies continued for many years. Charles Darwin's ideas nevertheless spread throughout the world and scientific progress eventually proved him right.

Similarly, the Church ended up dismissing any contradiction between the theory of evolution and faith, now considering that the intervention of God was made at the birth of the universe, to which he gave his laws. However, other more fanatical religious groups continue even today to deny the theory of Charles Darwin, preferring a literal reading of the Bible. These groups called creationists are mainly found in the United States and Australia.

DARWINISM AND NEO-DARWINISM

While staying away from debates, Charles Darwin neverthe-less continued his work and provided arguments supporting his theory as best he could. He thus made many other pu-blications that supported his claims or dealt with different subjects. Aware that he could not indefinitely avoid the sub-ject, the naturalist also tackled the question of man in *The Descent of Man, and Selection in Relation to Sex*, published in 1871, followed by *The Expression of the Emotions in Man and Animals* the following year. In these two books, Charles Darwin placed man among the mammals, which, like other species, had descended from a common ancestor. Man is also subject to evolution. However, the naturalist did not see man as the product of natural selection, but of another factor, namely sexual selection which, although less rigo-rous, also appeared in other species. The most handsome and strongest males were more likely to reproduce and have offspring.

Although heavily criticized, Charles Darwin also had some defenders, which could be found especially in the younger generation of naturalists who saw his work as revolutionary in the field of science. Darwinism, which defends the theory of evolution, was born. During the last years of Darwin's life and well after, many researchers continued his work. The question of man was still a debate, prompting many scientists to search for the missing link, hypothetically making the link between ape and man. In 1856, fossil remains of Neanderthals were found in Germany. Advocates of Darwin's theory were quick to see it as an earlier stage of human evolution. Later, in the 20th century, other fossils would also show the evolution of man, from *Homo erectus* to *Homo habilis*.

Meanwhile, in 1865, the precursor of genetics, Gregor Mendel (1822-1884), discovered the laws of heredity and genes, which reinforced the theory of evolution, although Darwin had not been aware of these theories. In the early 20th century, Mendel's works were paralleled to the theory of evolution, giving rise to Neo-Darwinism or "modern evolutionary synthesis". Complemented by genetics, Darwin's theory became inevitable and perfectly explained the transmission of variations from one individual to their offspring. Genetics and the discovery of DNA research also disrupted research on human evolution. Scientists discovered that man was a cousin to the ape, not a direct descendant. The search for the missing link stopped in favor of the oldest ancestor common to men and apes.

Although Charles Darwin died on 19 April 1872, his groundbreaking book still remains one of the major works of history, deeply marking the sciences and philosophical conceptions of nature and species, including humans. "Whilst this planet has gone circling on according to the fixed law of gravity, from so simple a beginning endless forms most beautiful and most wonderful have been, and are being evolved." (Darwin 2008).

SUMMARY

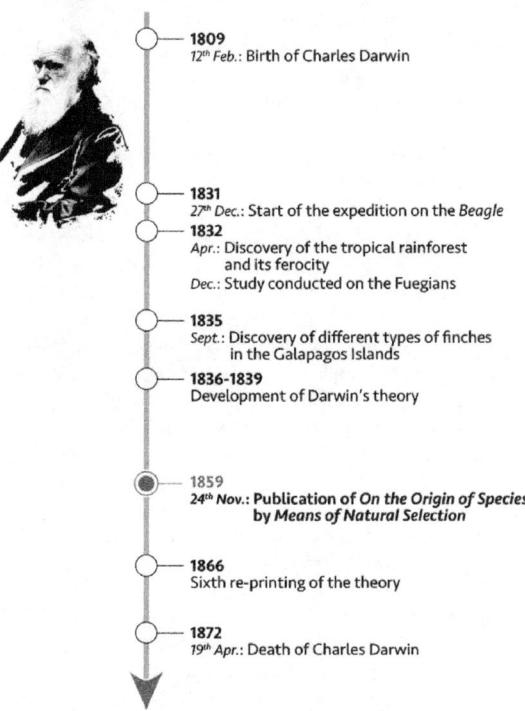

1809
12th Feb.: Birth of Charles Darwin

1831
27th Dec.: Start of the expedition on the *Beagle*

1832
Apr.: Discovery of the tropical rainforest
    and its ferocity
Dec.: Study conducted on the Fuegians

1835
Sept.: Discovery of different types of finches
    in the Galapagos Islands

1836-1839
Development of Darwin's theory

1859
24th Nov.: **Publication of *On the Origin of Species***
    by Means of Natural Selection

1866
Sixth re-printing of the theory

1872
19th Apr.: Death of Charles Darwin

- Charles Darwin was born on 12 February 1809 in England.
  A poor student, he began studying to become a doctor

and pastor, but with no real interest in doing so. However, he was passionate about the natural sciences and undertook a collection of plants and insects.

- At the end of his studies, the young man had the opportunity to participate in the expedition of the *Beagle* around the world as a naturalist. Accepting the offer, he began his journey on 27 December 1831. This trip led to Charles Darwin becoming a renowned naturalist.

- In April 1832, he discovered the rainforest and was shocked by the ferocity of nature and the struggle between the different species to survive. This vision was far removed from the idea of a bountiful nature according to divine will. This experience forever changed Darwin's thinking.

- The *Beagle* reached Tierra del Fuego in December 1832. By studying the tribes of Tierra del Fuego, Darwin saw his ideas on the origin of man completely disrupted. He did not see man as being separate from and above other animals, but as a mammal like any other.

- The expedition then reached the Galapagos Islands in September 1835. On this archipelago, the young naturalist had the opportunity to admire evidence of speciation and variation of species through the finches, of which he discovered no less than 13 different types, differentiated by the size of their beaks.

- Back in England in 1836, Charles Darwin immediately began to analyze his notes and catalog his collection, even trusting some of the collections to several specialists in order to gather as much information as possible. Until 1839, he wrote books on his theory of evolution.

- Collecting as much evidence as he could, Darwin surrounded himself with many specialists and continued his research. He eventually laid the foundation of his theory by defining natural selection as the trigger for evolution and the struggle for survival as the driving force. However, concerned about the impact that such a disruption could cause, Charles Darwin took twenty years to write his book.

- After writing several drafts in 1842 and 1844, and finally beginning to actually write it in 1856, Charles Darwin was hurriedly pushed to complete the publication of his work. Another naturalist, Alfred Wallace, had reached the same result as him and there was a risk that he would publish his theory first.

- On 24 November 1859, the new theory of evolution was published under the name *On the Origin of Species by Means of Natural Selection*. The book was so successful that it was reprinted six times until 1866.

- Charles Darwin's book immediately provoked controversy, particularly among the representatives of the Church. The naturalist nevertheless continued his work and tackled the question of the origin of man and his evolution, forever shattering the philosophical ideas of his time.

- Charles Darwin died on 19 April 1872.

We want to hear from you!
Leave a comment on your online library
and share your favourite books on social media!

FIND OUT MORE

BIBLIOGRAPHY

- Bowlby, J. (1992) *Charles Darwin: A New Life*. New York: W.W. Norton & Company.
- Brosse, J. (1999) *Les tours du monde des explorateurs. Les grands voyages maritimes, 1764-1843*. Paris: Bordas.
- Continenza, B. (2004) *Darwin, l'arbre de vie*. Paris: Pour la Science.
- Darwin, C. (2002) *Autobiographies*. London: Penguin.
- *Darwin, C. (2008) On the Origin of Species. Oxford : Oxford World's Classics.*
- Histoire universelle : le XIXe siècle en Europe et en Amérique du Nord (2007) *Création de l'Empire britannique*. Paris: Hachette.
- Histoire universelle : le XIXe siècle en Europe et en Amérique du Nord (2007) *La science romantique*. Paris: Hachette.
- Histoire universelle : le XIXe siècle en Europe et en Amérique du Nord (2007) *Positivisme et science expérimentale*. Paris: Hachette.
- Rice, T. (1999) *Voyages : trois siècles d'explorations naturalistes*. Neuchâtel: Delachaux and Niestlé.
- Tort, P. (1997) *Darwin et le darwinisme*. Paris: Presses Universitaires de France.

ADDITIONAL SOURCES

- Desmond, A. Moore, J.A. (1992) *Darwin*. New York: W.W. Norton & Company.

- Ruse, M. (2008) *Charles Darwin*. Oxford: Blackwell.
- Ruse, M. (eds.) (2013) *The Cambridge Encyclopedia of Darwin and Evolutionary Thought*. Cambridge: Cambridge University Press.
- Ruse, M. and Richards, R.J. (2016) *Debating Darwin*. Chicago: University of Chicago Press.
- Strager, H. (2016) *A Modest Genius: The Story of Darwin's Life and How His Ideas Changed Everything*. CreateSpace Independent Publishing Platform.

ICONOGRAPHIC SOURCES

- Voltaic pile, image from the book *Leçons de Physique* by Louise Margat-L'Huillier. Paris: Vuibert et Nony, 1904. Royalty-free reproduction picture.
- Carl Linnaeus, engraving from the book *Famous Men of Science* by Sarah K. Bolton. New York: T. Y. Crowell & Co., 1889. Royalty-free reproduction picture.
- *Charles Darwin at age 7,* by Ellen Sharples, 1816. Royalty-free reproduction picture.
- Alfred Russel Wallace, 1908. Royalty-free reproduction picture.
- *Le HMS Beagle in Tierra del Fuego by* Conrad Martens. This painting was produced during the *Beagle*'s journey (1831-1836). Royalty-free reproduction picture.
- Darwin's finches, 1845. © John Gould.

FILMS AND DOCUMENTARIES

- *Darwin et la Science de l'évolution*. (2003) [Documentary]. Valérie Winckler. Dir. France: Arte

France, Trans Europe Film, CNRS Images.
- *Charles Darwin and the Tree of Life.* (2009) [Documentary]. David Attenborough. Writ. UK: British Broadcasting Corporation, The Open University.
- *Creation.* (2009) [Film]. Jon Amiel. Dir. UK: Recorded Picture Company.
- *Le Grand Voyage de Charles Darwin.* (2009) [Documentary]. Hannes Schuler and Katharina von Flotow. Dir. France: Les Films du Paradoxe.

MUSEUMS AND COMMEMORATIVE MONUMENTS

- Down House, the house of Charles Darwin, Down, Kent (United Kingdom).
- Charles Darwin monument, Shrewsbury (United Kingdom).
- Natural History Museum, London (United Kingdom).
- Statue of Charles Darwin at the Natural History Museum, London (United Kingdom).

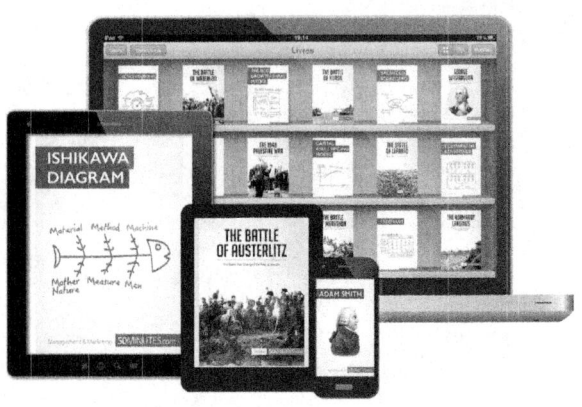